**winner
michigan writers cooperative press
2024 creative nonfiction contest**

Brain Aura Blues
Melissa Seitz

Copyright © 2024 by Melissa Seitz. All rights reserved.

Michigan Writers Cooperative Press
P. O. Box 2355
Traverse City, Michigan 49685

ISBN-13: 978-1-950744-18-3

Book cover by Amy Hansen
Book interior by Daniel Stewart

Contents

Framed	1
Where are you?	3
In Your Head	6
The Incredibly Shrinking Meningioma	11
Running Down a Dream	14
The Sky is Crying	16
Dreaming of Dead People: The Underbelly of Dark Dreams	19
You Can't Always Get What You Want	21
Blues Before Sunrise	24
Walking Blues	25
Waiting Is the Hardest Part	28
Brain Damage	31
Taking Care of Business	33
Acknowledgements	39
About the Nonfiction Judge	40
About the Author	41
About Michigan Writers Cooperative Press	42
Other Titles Available	43

For Jim and Matt
In memory of Nicole

BRAIN AURA BLUES

Framed

I remember the first time I saw the Gamma Knife machine. Badass. It reminded me of a giant monster's eyeball that I was about to enter and disappear into. I winced at the sound of the name, and I wanted to call my mother. She had been dead for over three years, the Alzheimer's mangling her brain into inoperative matter. My father, still very much alive at the age of 91, joined my husband and son to watch my head get zapped on the closed-circuit television in the hospital. No station breaks for advertising. My revolution would be televised, but there would be no sudden interruptions where the local weatherman warned the viewing audience that a tornado was about to take the roof off a house or a blizzard was about to bury an entire city in a foot of snow. November could be a tricky month. I could have cared less. My brain was about to be fried.

The first insult to my ego had been at the hair salon the day before. I told Diane, my stylist who knew me better than anyone, to chop off my long blonde hair. I had no idea what 54 minutes of radiation might do. Although the days of my platinum, over-dyed, look-at-me, waist-length hair were over, I still took pride in looking somewhat attractive for my age. "Chop it," I said. "Are you sure?" Diane asked while holding the scissors as if in prayer. "Do it." With that, she snipped away. My chopped-off hair fell on the floor like clumps of dry spiderwebs. When she finished, I looked closely into the oversized mirror. Alvin the Chipmunk winked back at me.

The second insult to my self-esteem was when the nurses put

the stereotactic helmet on my head and screwed it in. Not only did it hurt as if someone had given my head four quick blows with a hammer, but I was also informed that I had to wear the six-pound helmet before, during, and for a little while after the surgery. For someone with a head my size, and I had always been sensitive about this, I had no idea that weight displacement in proportion with skull circumference did not matter. I was glad that my long hair had been eliminated from all this dramatic bullshit.

The third insult to my self-confidence was when they rolled me into the room for the surgery. For some reason, the room reminded me of the exact hospital room where my daughter had died four days after being born. Had they repurposed the room? She had been dead since 1988. This was 2011. I knew the hospital had remodeled many areas. Was there a connection? Was I losing my mind? Nicole died because her brain did not work—anencephaly—and now I was in a similar room with my own damn brain issues. Perhaps this would be the room I would die in.

One of the technicians slid me into the Gamma Knife machine and the collimator helmet came down over my stereotactic frame as if I were a victim in *The Night of The Living Dead*. For fifty-four minutes, I was not allowed to move. The doctors targeted the meningioma. They would not aim the radiation at my whacked-out sense of humor. They would not destroy my love of blues music. They would not make me forget my grief. They would not reach into my soul and my heart and shatter the depth of love that I had for my family.

I had been allowed to create the perfect brain surgery playlist. In the control room, where they were preparing everything for my date with radiation, Larry, my new favorite DJ, spoke to me over the headphones. "I'm going to start your music." Party on. Let Stevie Ray Vaughan, Ray LaMontagne, Grace Potter, and other musicians I had selected entertain me as the Gamma Knife rays worked their magic. Shrink that meningioma. I was ready.

Where are you?

Your mouth forms an "m" for Marquette, but you cannot speak the word. Language dissolves somewhere in your brain like water evaporating on hot pavement. You sip your beer with unsteady hands and wonder if it is your last one. You stare wildly at your husband and your friends. You stretch your brain for a moment. Good. You know their names, but you cannot say them. Where have your words gone? You have the worst migraine of your life.

Your husband stares at you with his dark green eyes, his mustache forming a wavering river of worry. He repeats his question. "Where are you?"

Your lips form the "m" again, but you shake your head. You aren't sure. Are you in Marquette? Midland? Mexico? Manitoba?

You wonder why the sun is so fucking bright inside the restaurant and particularly above your friend George's head who sits directly across from you. The aura sneers at you as if you are standing helpless in the middle of the road, and a one-eyed semi is headed straight for you. You duck and turn toward your right where your friend Julie sits. Her hair reminds you of red licorice. She tries to comfort you and holds one of your hands as if you were a child.

Your turn to your husband and say, "Going red." Everyone stands up and insists on taking you to the hospital. You refuse to go and plant yourself firmly in your chair. "Blue," you say. You have no idea what you mean by these words. They sit down. You are scared out of your mind.

You wonder if your meningioma is growing inside your head

again, the ugly bastard of a brain tumor. Your husband brings up the ER again, but you shake your head. No, no, no. You have lost your words before, forgotten names that go with faces, but they have all come back to you in time. You were scared then, too. But this is public. Fuck. Fuck. You can think of that word, but you cannot say it. You want to scream it.

Time passes, and your mouth slowly begins to work again. "I have to go to the bathroom." The words fly out of your mouth like confetti. You walk down the stairs of the Delft Bistro. Somewhere in the bowels of the building you hear an old blues song, but you aren't sure if it is real. Is anything?

In the delicate light of the bathroom, you stare into the mirror and try to remember the woman you used to be before the meningioma. Before the grand mal seizure. Before the gamma knife surgery to reduce the size of the tumor. Before the wires got crossed in your damaged brain. You try and remember yourself before your daughter died.

You climb back up the stairs and return to your seat. You pick at your steak salad, no longer hungry. You swallow the dregs of your beer. You reassure everyone you will be just fine. You do not believe a word of it.

When you, your husband, George, and Julie leave the restaurant, complete strangers eye you carefully as you walk by. Your brain hurts as if it is 1973 again and you have just smoked a wicked joint, and cannot find your way home. Still, you will your body forward.

Later, back at the hotel, your husband, the researcher, will tell you that you might have suffered from transient aphasia. By chance or luck or fate, you have an appointment with your neurosurgeon and an MRI coming up the following week to check on the stupid meningioma. You have so many questions.

How convenient.

It's September 2023. In your hotel room that evening, you and your husband sit near the window. The September cold seeps through the glass as you watch the almost full moon rise above Lake Superior. "I should be outside taking pictures, but I am so tired," you say. You run the words to "Moondance" and "Mr. Moonlight" through your head. You could sing those songs if you wanted to, but you sit back, watch the blue hour surround the Lower Harbor, and wait.

In Your Head

For my eighth MRI in the last twelve years, I lay flat on my back on the scanning table waiting for my head to be rolled towards the MRI's powerful magnet and into the giant metal and plastic donut hole. Although I had been to the Grayling Hospital many times over the years for all kinds of things, it was my first time at this particular hospital for an MRI.

"I guess I don't need to explain things," the technician joked.

I laughed and tried not to sound jaded. "How old is this one?" I pointed above and behind my head as if for clarity. The complex machine was very similar to other ones I had slid into.

I always worried about my head being scrunched into the opening, because, with a little less than 24 inches, there didn't seem to be much margin for error. I had been sensitive about the size of my head since I discovered that one-size-fits-all hats do not. I used an open MRI machine twice in Midland, Michigan, to help battle my claustrophobia, but I wasn't convinced of its efficacy. Where exactly were those magnetic images going?

"Sixteen years," Nick replies. "We were due for a new one and then COVID hit."

Ah, yes, the old COVID alibi, excuse, reason, whatever. COVID changed a lot of things, killed a few friends, and finally caught up to me and my family. Luckily, our son Matt, myself, and my husband passed it around to each other at the same time. Jim had it the worst: he had just gotten out of the Gaylord hospital after major abdominal surgery. He coughed like he was riding a roller coaster during a thunderstorm.

"What do you want on your playlist?" Nick asked.

I was prepared for this question and requested my go-to genre, classic rock. For one of my MRIs in Midland, they played country. I wondered how they confused the two. Perhaps a technician hit the wrong button. That had been concerning. During my first two MRIs, no music played. Hell, I didn't remember them at all. An entire marching band could have been playing next to my left ear, all trombones and tubas, and I would not have heard a sound.

My introduction to the world of MRIs began the day I had been running in a Halloween zombie run. After two miles, the sky split into shades of gray, and then disappeared. I'd suffered a grand mal seizure.

When I came to, I was surrounded by zombies, Santa Claus, and a few people who seemed to be humans, all staring down at me. I felt as if I were looking through a periscope into the gates of hell. I thought I had died. After an ambulance ride to the Traverse City Hospital, I began a brand-new adventure with a lot of tests involving bulky machinery. Surprise! That was only the beginning. Welcome to your meningioma nightmare!

"Here we go," the technician said after adjusting my headphones. He smiled as he slid me into the chamber.

"Wait. I need a washcloth." I had learned that placing one over my eyes helped my claustrophobia.

Nick returned quickly, placed the washcloth over the head coil, and quickly locked me into place. He exited the large area and entered his secure room, safe from the powerful magnetic fields and high-frequency radio waves. He spoke to me through the headphones. His voice sounded much more soothing in stereo as he asked me if I was ready.

"Ready," I said.

The thumps and bangs prevented me from hearing the first unfamiliar song clearly. Skid Row's song "I Remember You" popped into my mind from radio-nowhere past. Classic rock? What? I listened to the song, sort of between the bang-bang-bang-bang and the boom-boom-booms. I tried to control my breathing.

I drifted off slightly and felt the clinginess of anxiety creep in. I wanted to scratch somewhere around my neck just to feel some movement in my body. The fingers of my right-hand inched up slowly towards my throat. It felt cool, alive.

One of the basic rules was not to move. What would happen if I had a coughing fit? Farted? Threw up? I smiled at my ridiculousness.

I blanked out song two and song three began. I was stunned. "Zombie" by the Cranberries blasted through the lousy headphones. What the hell? It's not Halloween. A few days before, we had heard this song in the car when we returned from Marquette. Jim drove. I rode shotgun, and George and Julie sat in the backseat. For almost five hours, George and I took turns playing DJ. Via my phone and the car stereo system, George picked a song, and I fired it up. Then I picked a song and hit play. George had selected an acoustic version of "Zombie" by the Cranberries which I had never heard before. It was eerily beautiful. Now, as I remained flat on my back listening to the Cranberries sing the more familiar version, I wanted to laugh hysterically.

Of course, "Zombie" was about so much more than my stupid head. O'Riordan wrote the song as a protest number after young boys were killed in IRA bombings in England in 1993. I understood the significance of the song. But now, I only saw how it related to my situation. O'Riordan's powerful singing, yodeling, and lamenting made me want to rise off the table and tell the technician to stop the banging noises for a moment. We needed to listen to the music. Clearly. Quietly. Respectfully. I wanted to turn back time for so many reasons.

But the song ended. I took a breath, but not too deeply so as not to disrupt the machine. A few more songs played, but I had begun thinking of other things.

The technician announced over the headphones, "It's time for your injection." He entered the room and injected the contrast solution into my arm. The routine was so familiar that I made small talk about the size of my almost invisible veins. The metallic taste hit my mouth and the noises fired up again after the technician left. Nirvana's "Come as You Are" roared through the clunking noises of the machine.

I was flabbergasted. Really? Classic rock? Where were Led Zeppelin and Pink Floyd? Did they consider them ancient rock? Or geezers rock? This playlist stunk. I swore silently in the name of rock and roll.

A Bon Jovi song came on the playlist, and he wailed about not living forever and making the most of each day and every day. I thought of a woman a few years younger than myself. We stood in her warm kitchen, the scent of something I couldn't understand still ripe between us. She looked at me carefully and repeated words she had said a year earlier to me: "You should be living your life." She seemed mad about something.

It was the second time she had informed me that I was doing something wrong. I didn't even know her that well. Yet, she had judged me, handed out a verdict, and sent me on my way. I had been too stunned to inquire what she meant.

Booms and bangs from the machine suddenly snapped me out of my mood. An MRI always gave me too much time to think. I sighed and hoped I hadn't moved too much.

A few more songs played, but either my mind was blocking out the crappy tunes, or I just didn't care. It wasn't real classic rock. The beat of the MRI reminded me of something, maybe Led Zeppelin's "When the Levee Breaks." I smiled. "In-A-Gadda-Da-Vidda" by Iron Butterfly would be perfect. What I really desired was some good old blues music. Some B.B. King singing "After the Thrill is Gone" or John Lee Hooker daring me to "Chill Out (Things Gonna Change)" would have eased my mind a whole lot better.

Nick interrupted my thoughts: "All done." His voice sounded like a smooth Wolfman Jack.

I stretched and moved slowly as he slid me back out into the reality of the room. I rose cautiously from the scanning bed, noted the gigantic red sign that cautioned STOP, asked him for a copy of the disk, and told him I would wait. I thanked him and entered the changing room. After finishing up, I met Nick outside the small cubicle, and he guided me towards the exit. In the waiting room, Jim broke into a mustache-covered grin when he saw me.

"How was it?" he asked.

"The same. You won't believe what song they played." I bent down to give him a kiss. "Zombie."

We smiled at each other, sat down, and waited for the newest version of the rest of my life.

The Incredibly Shrinking Meningioma

After the Gamma Knife surgery, I began referring to 2012 as the year that really sucked. I became ornery as hell, but at least I owned it. My brain tumor was conveniently located right where my emotions, language, and memories hang out. I imagined the meningioma squishing everything together and creating havoc just to piss me off. I had to run so I wouldn't crash and burn.

I stood on the sidewalk in downtown Midland with my dear friend Darcy after doing a bit of shopping, just like in the old days when I still lived there. I tried to avoid places where I might run into someone I used to know. I was not always successful.

"So, you are all better now, right?" The woman asked, her blueish-green jacket reminding me of a peacock in full bloom. She smiled.

"Right," I said and beamed back at her. I felt my right hand clench momentarily, and then I quickly released it before stretching my fingers as if I had a cramp. I knew she meant well. After all, no one could see my brain tumor. So why would it be an issue? But after that uncomfortable encounter, I learned that ducking behind sunflowers at the farmers market was a foolproof method for avoidance.

I was reminded of my overwhelming grief when Nicole died. No one could see my broken heart so, if they saw me out in the world, people seemed to think I was fine. One day I finally mustered up the courage to be around a bunch of children again, and decided to pick Matt up from kindergarten. The mother of one of the other kids walked up to me and said, "Welcome back." Did she think I had been on vacation? I avoided her as much as possible for the next six years.

How long was grief supposed to last? A month? A year? Five years? Ten? Twenty? Until a person died seemed right to me. And my meningioma? So many people appeared to think that if they could not see my brain tumor, then it must be fine. But I had to live with a brain tumor stuck in my head, just like I lived each and every day with the grief about Nicole's death. I tried to convince myself that I did not have any problems, but it just made things worse.

During those first two horrible years with my Stupid Brain Tumor, as I referred to it, my memory resembled garbled mash. Thankfully, because I loved writing, I kept a journal and wrote down just about everything. I became the Memory Keeper for myself.

My dreams revolved around musicians: I dreamt of meeting George Harrison. On another night, I pushed Eric Clapton around in a wheelchair. I dreamt of doing shots with Vince Gill. And my dreams were violent. In one, I dreamt of former Red Wings hockey player Sergei Federov being murdered in a fancy mansion. In another one, people were bleeding in an office. One dream came uncomfortably close to something that could happen in my future. I was in a nursing home. A tornado was headed straight for me, and I was forced to bust out and run for it. Dreams like this convinced me I needed to write. Death, music, sunrise, and nature were constant themes.

The medication I was on created huge holes in my memory. It helped prevent me from having another life-threatening seizure, but swallowing those pills twice a day basically erased my memory.

I began crying a lot. In fact, my emotions were completely out of control, and it seemed as if I were watching the movies *Beaches*, *Steel Magnolias*, and *Terms of Endearment* on repeat. At other times, I sobbed for no discernible reason. I would then run to my husband and beg him to tell me that I was still funny. He acted as if he wasn't surprised, wiped my ugly tears with his T-shirt, hugged me, kissed me with his sexy mustache, and assured me that I was hilarious. Strangely, I believed him. With that, I would return to my Woman Cave and watch six episodes of NCIS reruns in a row. I had a crush on Mark Harmon and Cote De Pablo. Mark was a handsome dude I liked to look at, and I wanted to kick ass like Cote. Anyone's ass.

The end of 2011 and all of 2012 were tough years. The grand mal seizure during the Halloween Zombie Run in Traverse City kicked things off. Then, the following July, my beloved dog died at the age of seventeen. My father died the following month at the age of 92. I wondered what in the hell I had done in the universe to deserve the wrath of God, friends, and anyone else, for that matter.

When Nicole had died in 1988 and people suddenly started avoiding me because dead children were so difficult to talk about, I spent time in the hallway of our small ranch house in Midland. There were no pictures on the walls. No one could see if I was home. I did not have to speak to anyone if I did not want to. Eventually, I started running to cope.

I remember putting on my pink running shoes and walking up the hill to the end of our driveway at Higgins Lake. I looked both ways and wondered which way I should go. Whichever way I went, I would carry the weight of my meningioma and my grief with me. I knew I was a badass though. I wasn't better yet. Hell, I might never be. But I was trying to get there one step at a time.

Running Down a Dream

The crushing grip of grief and trauma have taught me many things. When I have pain, I do something to make myself feel better. When Nicole died, I chose running. Eventually, through injuries and aging, I switched to power walking. I still run occasionally for two or three miles just to prove I can. I raise my fist at the end of the route as if to show the world that I can still do it, no matter what.

I have had people question me about my knees, age, and craziness when I head out on the roads. Icy pavements and strong winds seem especially concerning to others, but not to me. I love to say that I recently finished an eight-or-nine miler as I gulp down an orange Gatorade. I sometimes wonder how sane I really am. I hope like hell to drop dead during a road race as some sort of ultimate grief response. I am still trying to work this out in my head.

I love distance races, but feel too old now for a full marathon. The longest ones I have run or power walked are half marathons. My body keeps sending me messages after eight-mile races or nine-mile training workouts. Afterwards, my muscles require longer periods of stretching and bouts with my foam roller to scrub the bursitis in my right leg. I had surgery on my leg after the doctors discovered a tear and all sorts of ugliness from a different sort of MRI. Like a fool, I had continued running even when I could barely walk. My head was as screwed up as my leg.

My meningioma announced itself in the most spectacular way about two miles into the zombie race. I began jerking, moaning, groaning, dropping to the ground, banging my head, and eventually losing consciousness. The grand-mal seizure, now known as a tonic-clonic seizure, sure got everyone's attention. Thankfully, I have no memory of it. My body, amazingly, weathered this fairly well. My head, however, suffered a large bump on the outside. The inside of my head had a bad-girl party of its own.

When I regained consciousness during the race, surrounded by zombies, other runners, a doctor, and emergency personnel, I quickly realized that I was in a lot of trouble. I assumed that I was going to die. "An extraordinary fall," they called it. I woke up in the hospital for the second time after a surreal ambulance ride. My memories were jumbled. Darcy and her husband showing up—they had been running the race, too. More people standing around and looking at me with worried looks. My husband driving from home, Matt coming up from Midland, and all of us bursting into tears at the sight of each other. I was scared shitless.

The next morning, a nurse walked me down the hall to watch the sunrise out of a fairly large window. I knew I had a lot to think about. We discussed my options with the doctors. I had to do something. They sent me on my way. In the end, I chose Gamma Knife surgery. The other option, cutting my head open to remove the tumor, was riskier and the wait, longer.

During recovery, grief started rearing its ugly head in my waking hours and dreams. I stood on the beach in front of our house at Higgins Lake and wondered how far out I could swim in the crystal-clear water before I began sinking. I had to remind myself that I had suffered trauma, and that I was on intense medication to prevent seizures. My sadness played me like a Celine Dion song. I wanted to be funny again.

My grief for Nicole had been tucked somewhere inside for so long that it was as if something had erupted through my skin and become visible. The deaths of my daughter, my mother, my dog, and then my father had seemingly built a wall around my emotions. Something burst.

The Sky is Crying

Two years after my brain surgery, my then neurologist scheduled an EEG for me to see if it would be possible to reduce the dosage for my anti-seizure medication. A few weeks later, a technician hooked me up as if I were some greasy-haired Medusa and ran tests to see what would happen. When my doctor discussed the results with me and my husband, I sat back and listened. Here he was, in his very sharp suit, talking about my wacky brain as if he was telling me it was going to rain tomorrow.

"A seizure would still be a slight possibility," he said.

My heart sunk. Since the woman who had done my EEG said she could see brain damage, I asked how my brainwaves worked near the brain tumor and where the radiation had burned a hole in my head. I thought this was funny.

The doctor said, "The EEG showed a distinctly different pattern when the brainwaves were churning through the 'damaged' zone." To hell with my brain. The doctor meant well. He did not want me to freak out about my brain damage. He slightly reduced the dosage of my medication and encouraged me to go out there and live my life. Of course, it wouldn't be until years later that a woman standing in her kitchen would tell me that I should be living my life. And all this time, I thought I had been. Despite my brain damage, excruciating migraines, and the weight of grief I carried with me wherever I went, I thought I was doing a hell of a job.

Yet, there was this expectation when I walked out the door that I should act as if I was fine. I should not upset people. I have noticed over the years that talking about grief and life trauma seemed to make a lot of people uncomfortable around me. Only a few of my closest friends stop what they are doing and listen when I am having a horrible day. I love them desperately.

As for the other people who dismiss me or don't want to hear that I went to my daughter's grave to place flowers on a cold and dreary day, I get it. They probably have their own grief, and they aren't willing to explore it yet. I was there once. I was so afraid to open the door of heartbreak that I threw away the key. I began running to save myself.

After the grand mal seizure, people started telling me how lucky I was to be alive. I felt nauseated every time I heard the word. Yes, I knew I was lucky I had the big-ass seizure during a road race, and a doctor was running next to me. I also knew I could have been running alone down an isolated road near my house, dropped on the pavement, and choked to death. I could have been driving and ended up far off in the woods just off Fletcher Road between my house and Traverse City. I tried to explain my fears, but people reminded me that it didn't happen that way. I was lucky. I wanted to shout at them, "You don't understand."

I read books about memory and grief to see if they would jump start my brain. I had to take notes as if I were in college again. My damaged brain somehow found new pathways to send information through, but it didn't seem as efficient as before. I wrote depressing poetry about my mother. "I imagined her waving at me one last time / as if the small movement of her hand would always save me." And on it sadly went. Thankfully, music pulled me through, and I could remember the lyrics from every song I ever loved.

I began to understand some things about myself, but it took years and the encouragement of family and friends. I continued getting MRIs. I went to writers' workshops and wrote banal essays and poems. At least I tried. Wonderful people encouraged me. My friend Chris told me to send him anything I wrote, and he would provide feedback. I did. He did.

I ran ten to twenty road races a year. They made me feel so

very much alive. I trained almost every day. Thunderstorms and snowstorms were the only things that kept me off the roads. To cope, I started watching *Dexter* reruns, a show about a vigilante serial killer. I also began reading books about serial killers. I was in a very dark place.

One day in late 2018, Chris suggested that I should attend a writing workshop about grief. So I did. For many months, I went to the sessions and wrote about grief with other people who also felt like torturing their souls. It would take me a long, long time to understand that I was learning to own my grief. Or as Joanne Cacciatore, PHD, says in her book, *Bearing the Unbearable*, I was "defending the dignity of my grief" (29).

Grief, just like my Stupid Brain Tumor, lived inside my head, and my body somehow carried me wherever I went. The scars of grieving refused to fade. The fractures within me framed my history silently, but when they needed to release steam, they did. When I ran or power walked, I was screaming down the road.

Dreaming of Dead People: The Underbelly of Dark Dreams

While you wait for the test results from your latest MRI, napping becomes your escape from reality. You dream of a boy you barely knew in high school named Richie. You had lost touch with him and heard that he died in 2007. In your dream, he is seventeen with long blonde hair slinking down over his startlingly bluish-green eyes. You ask him questions in dream gibberish.

You lost track of him after high school. Why is he returning to you now?

Perhaps Richie has been on your mind because you missed your high school reunion in 2023. The year he died, you lived in Michigan, worked full time, and cared for your mother who was sick and dying from Alzheimer's. Your father attempted to care for her, but ended up having a lot of health problems of his own. You saw your husband in the evenings as you both collapsed on the couch with your dog cuddled up between you. Your son, grown up and on his own after graduating with his master's degree in civil engineering, lived in his own apartment. His bedroom looked confusing to you then without all his belongings scattered on the dresser and bed. You ran when you could to keep yourself sane. You silently grieved the death of your daughter every single day. This was four years before the brain tumor knocked you down, flat on your ass.

What had Richie's story been before he died? Some of his old friends would know. But for now, you would just let him be what he was in your dream: young and beautiful. You think of the dream again, and how you had asked him to come with you. He said he could not leave. It was at that point you realized you had to get out of wherever he was. You weren't ready.

When you entered sweet awareness as you awakened from your deep, dark afternoon sleep, you remembered the color of Richie's hair, pulled a wisp of it with you as you slipped into wakefulness, and waited for your eyes to adjust to the weight of the world. You wondered why people returned to you at different times in your life within your dreams or your thoughts. You were used to your parents and your daughter, Nicole, but when strangers appeared, you were never quite sure how to handle or decipher the message. Maybe it was something as simple as a desire to be young again, to walk down the hall of Dodge City Senior High School in your bell bottoms and peasant top, and say hello to Richie and look closely at the color of his eyes.

You Can't Always Get What You Want

Jim and I were prepared for our Facetime call with the neurosurgeon. We were in my office among my overstuffed bookshelves, an acoustic guitar, hearts made from glass, wood, and rocks, and thirty-five years of race medals that hung from two separate racks that sloppily overflowed. Plaques, a cowbell, a growler, and other assorted prizes I had won for placing first, second, or third in my age group during races lined different shelves. Photos of Matt, Nicole, Jim, my parents, and special friends filled up other spaces on shelves. My Woman Cave was difficult to clean.

I sat at my desk, and Jim was next to me on a barstool. He had researched everything there was to know about MRI results and transient aphasia. He was always a much better student than I. He had pages and pages of notes. I had jotted down a few questions, and I suddenly felt as if I had failed to prepare for the test.

We both had read the results a week earlier in my patient portal online. Still, we wanted to hear the official report from the doctor. I had said the same prayer during every sunrise meditation: *Please, no surprises.*

I had so many questions about migraines and aphasia. I wondered if something more sinister lurked inside my brain. My last MRI had been in June of 2022, which had been a little over a year ago. Why was I suddenly writing so much? What did exercise have to do with my headaches? Electrolytes?

The phone rang, but it wasn't Facetime. I informed the doctor that I expected a face-to-face call. She seemed surprised, hung up, and called back five minutes later. She explained that she could not do a Facetime call. I reminded her that she had Facetimed with me last year. She seemed flustered, so I decided to move on. Jim and I rolled our eyes at each other. At least she couldn't see us.

She told us that my MRI was fine, and that I wouldn't need another one for two or three years. The report confirmed well-defined calcification around the tumor which was a good thing. I asked a few basic questions, and I was shocked when she said she didn't know anything about my past history. I was immediately angry, and Jim sat up straighter on his barstool. We knew that she should have all my information. I reminded her that I had provided it the previous year. She did not reply. Jim then asked about additional cognitive testing that she had mentioned last year, and she said she didn't recall that either. Jim and I rolled our eyes at each other once again.

I asked about transient aphasia. She laughed and informed us that neurosurgeons don't talk about migraines or transient aphasia. Jim and I were surprised. We had written down several questions in my patient portal about my episode, and her team had responded to this by telling me to go to the ER if it happened again.

She said, "You need to get to your neurologist. Someone on my team should have told you that." She was sorry.

I was angry that she wasn't telling me that to my face.

After I hung up, Jim said, "She didn't even seem to know anything about you."

"No. I'm calling Dr. K. I'm done with her."

I told myself to breathe and stretched my neck. I selected my neurologist's number in my contacts and called his office. I explained my issue. The scheduler had a spot for me in five days.

I had waited and wasted over a week to get some answers and hopefully prevent another episode of transient aphasia or whatever it was. I was grateful for my husband's research. I planned to pay better attention if I felt as if I was entering the prodrome—the symptoms that preclude a migraine. I had to prepare myself for the worst-case scenario.

I looked at the old MRI picture of my meningioma I had on my photo board/calendar above my desk. My head in black and white looked odd. The golf-ball-sized blob inside the left part of my head really added some punch to the scan. No matter what happened next, I figured I would still get a prize for trying to stay one step ahead of whatever the days, months, and years I had left would bring. I might not always get what I wanted, but I might at least get something I needed.

Blues Before Sunrise

I was so used to running and power walking that I began to believe it was in my DNA somehow. I thrived on tearing up my body, feeling the hurt, reveling in the pain, and celebrating sweat dripping down my face. My endless miles of movement created endorphins that oozed throughout my body and somehow generated solace for my unseen heartache. I refused to believe I would ever have to slow down or come to a dead stop.

When I listened to music and watched the way the sun rose above the trees as I moved my body forward, I hoped to spot birds, especially eagles or hawks. I wanted them to fly directly over me, and bless me with their majestic wings as they continued their flight towards the great unknown. I always considered them as a sign from God. From Nicole. From the universe that wanted to keep me moving forward.

When I had leg surgery, I was briefly forced to stop running. I was slightly insane during that time. I worked harder than anyone in rehab and was back on the road in less than six weeks. I began my workouts doing circles in the driveway with hiking poles for support. I could not stand to be idle with my grief. I did not want to become stagnant again.

Walking Blues

As Jim drove me to my appointment with Dr. K. in Traverse City, I tried not to worry. I remarked on the reds, golds, and yellows of the leaves changing, understanding the significance of beauty before the breakdown and the decay.

Finally, we settled into a patient room in my neurologist's office. Dr. K. entered and listened intently as I explained my version of what went down during my "transient aphasia" episode. Jim's extensive Internet research had led me to this term. I also shared George and Julie's written version.

Jim then entered the conversation and described what he witnessed. I suddenly started to feel as if I was floating above the room listening to two grown men talk about me as if I wasn't even there. It was a strange but not unfamiliar feeling. It was as if I was under anesthesia and wanted to cry out that I could still feel the knife. This was my life they were discussing. Weren't my memories of the story the ones that mattered most?

Jim informed the doctor that I was talking gibberish during the episode. I liked that word, and I watched as Dr. K. wrote it down in long hand in his notebook. I liked that about him. Old school. Like me. Jim stated that they all wanted to take me to the ER, but I refused. Stubborn. He said that I could understand questions, but I could only respond with gibberish. There was that word again.

I jumped in and explained that I was scared to death. I wondered about the magical aura above George's head. It was so bright that I could not look at him. Dr. K. continued writing down more notes. He paused. Jim brought up the slight pattern I had of exercise-induced migraines and a brief discussion followed. Jim asked if this could be another possibility.

Dr. K. looked at me, considered, pondered, and thought some more while I awaited the verdict. The jury of one was out and then quickly back in again. He believed I had a complicated migraine. It was aphasia that was transient. He informed me that I needed to rule out other things. I suddenly felt the air escape through the closed door as if a balloon had just popped. Although I had been floating somewhere above the room in some sort of "are-they-talking-about-me" state, I immediately drifted downwards back into my chair.

"Let's schedule a carotid artery ultrasound to check the circulation of the large arteries in the neck where blood flows into the brain. Let's also schedule an EEG to look for strange brain activity which could indicate the possibility of a seizure." He said that my MRI had shown there was no evidence of a major stroke, but he wanted to assess the probability that a TIA or a mini-stroke might have been possible.

I sat back in my chair. I hadn't considered strokes. When I encountered obstacles in running, I dealt with them. Low boulders or impediments? I jumped over them. Mean dogs? I ran faster to escape them. Thunderstorms? I sought shelter. But a stroke? Or a series of mini-strokes? How did I deal with that?

I looked at the doctor and considered my options. I sighed. I asked if it was okay to power walk the Turtle Race on Mackinac Island on October 28th. Dr. K. leaned slightly forward in his chair as if I had just asked to borrow the keys to his car. He paused for a minute, looked at his notes, tilted his head, smiled, and said no.

I sat up straight in my chair and prepared my rebuttal, but he continued by explaining that I could not do anything strenuous until I received the results of my carotid artery ultrasound. If that test was normal, then I could go ahead and do the race without the results of the EEG. If I was at risk for a stroke or TIA, a road race was not a good idea. He looked at me to make sure I was paying attention. Jim looked at me sideways, his mustache giving off a detective vibe, like Magnum P.I. back in the day.

    I suddenly felt warm, grabbed my phone, and looked at my calendar. I had eleven days until the race. Wait. Wait. Wait. I stretched my neck, felt around the edges of it. Was trouble brewing there? Was it in my head? Was I just the queen of migraines?

Waiting Is the Hardest Part

This was no regular Friday night date. Jim drove as we headed towards Grayling Hospital for my carotid artery ultrasound appointment at 6:15 p.m. I was so stressed out that at one point I thought I had stopped breathing. I had convinced myself that my arteries were at least 90% blocked, and I would need surgery immediately. Forget complicated migraines. Worst-case scenarios had always been my go-to-thing, and I had filled my imaginary outsized shopping bag full of worrisome crap. I squirmed in my seat.

Halfway through the twenty-minute drive, I heard my late father say, "Stop worrying about it, Melissa. It won't do you any good." Shocked, I turned around to see if he had come back from the dead, wearing his ever-present brown beret covering his bald head. I couldn't tell if I was relieved or disappointed, because other than a box of Kleenex, the backseat was clear.

I glanced at Jim. He was focused on the road and didn't seem to notice anything unusual. I told him that I had just heard my father's voice from the backseat. He wasn't surprised. He was used to my frequent communications with the dead, especially my mother. I once heard her clear cool voice when I was in Kansas even though she had been dead for many years. I had been searching for information about our family history. Cardinals represented messages from all our parents. Hummingbirds represented Nicole with their tiny beauty. Spirituality came to me in many forms.

Jim shook his head as if he agreed with my father. "Don't worry about it. I think you will be fine."

I sat back in my seat and tried to relax. Jim pulled into the parking lot and I practically jumped out of the car. Since the main lobby door was closed, I entered through the emergency room door and checked in. After a brief bit of paperwork, I walked through the empty hallways towards the radiology waiting room. The cleaning lady was the only other person around. She eyed me as if I was just one more thing she had to deal with. I tried not to touch anything.

Eventually, the ultrasound technician, came out, apologized, asked me if I could wait, and explained that she was the only one there. She had an ER situation. I had no choice. I waited. She returned thirty minutes later, and I quickly followed her down the hall. I had been in the same hallway fourteen days ago for my MRI.

The technician led me to the room, explained what she was going to do, and informed me that I could not talk or snore. I was shocked. People fall asleep? I was suddenly frightened. According to my family, I snore like a semi downshifting from the top of a mountain. A very high mountain.

I wanted to watch, but I could only see the screen when she checked out the left side of my neck. The inside of my carotid artery looked weird, but I could at least see blood flowing and maybe something else. Aha, I thought. Trouble.

I asked the technician if she could share my results. I explained that I wanted to do a race the following Saturday on Mackinac Island. She said that she could not tell me anything, but the radiologist would look at the test that night or the next day. I asked if the results would be in the patient portal, my new best friend. Yes. I asked if I could figure out the results. Probably not. As I thanked her on the way out, she looked at me and said she hoped I would be able to do my race. I saw that as a sign.

As I entered the waiting room, Jim stood to greet me. As we headed for the exit, I explained the procedure to him. The cool breeze outside invigorated me after the dull antiseptic staleness of the hospital air. I had more waiting to do. I smiled as I wondered if my father would have any thoughts about this on the way home, but I didn't mention it to Jim. I climbed into the car and listened to the cool hum of the engine. I turned my head slightly, but I heard nothing from the backseat. I reached towards the radio and started to turn up a little Tom Petty on the radio, but I hesitated ... just in case.

Brain Damage

Seven days later, Jim drove me to the Grayling Hospital again for my one o'clock EEG appointment. Dr. K. had cleared me for the race since my carotid artery test results were normal, but he still wanted me to have an updated EEG. With little sleep and no caffeine, as required, I was groggy and grumpy. When I shot my sunrise photo earlier that morning, I swore the maple leaves and pine needles falling from the trees were out to get me. A loon's haunting wail out on the lake had echoed my frustration.

At the hospital, I kissed Jim goodbye and followed a cheerful young woman as she guided me down the hallway opposite from where I had my MRI and carotid artery test. Variety. How exciting. Sarcasm seemed the only way to cope.

The technician asked me the usual questions. I was thankful I still remembered my name and birthdate. I figured that someday I would fail this test. She placed a bright red cap with electrodes on my head with wires connected to a box. Those wires would make electrical contact with a nonmetallic part of a circuit while she recorded my brain waves into a computer. She added some extra green gel in a few places before she determined that I was fully connected. As she explained what would happen during the EEG, I hoped there would not be any power surges.

For the first part of my test, all I had to do was open and close my eyes. Easy. For the Photic Stimulation portion of the test, I closed my eyes and waited. The technician held a small box next to my head and flashed a series of lights in sequences of ten various flickering patterns. When she reached number five, I grabbed the side of the bedrail and felt nauseated. "Whoa," I said as if riding a horse. She offered to stop, but I said no. Sequences 8, 9, and 10 seemed like explosions behind my eyelids with kaleidoscopic bursts of gray and white matter. When she finished, I slowly opened my eyes.

Unlike the ultrasound a week earlier, the EEG included a sleep portion. But when it began, my brain refused to cooperate. I crawled towards sleep in my mind, watched the dream visions approach, saw a face in black and white, then a disappearing edge of a forest, and then nothing. I was cold. I heard the slight noise of the computer. I needed silence. Or blues music. I apologized for not falling asleep.

The technician informed me that changes in my brain waves were obvious during Photic Stimulation, and I wasn't surprised. When I had my EEG in 2014, my then neurologist had explained my "brain damage" to me, and how my brain waves danced around the tumor as if confused. The words "brain damage" had startled me. He had reminded me that I was lucky to be alive.

The technician guided me out the door, and I headed to the waiting room. Jim broke into a huge grin as soon as he saw me. He stared at my forehead and pointed towards two red circular marks where the EEG cap had been. I laughed, rubbed them, and made the marks worse. I covered my forehead with my hands as we walked outside.

I settled into the car and announced my desire for chocolate. Jim motioned toward the backseat where two smaller bags were inside a larger grocery bag. I ripped one of them open, grabbed two dark chocolate mint squares, my favorite, and quickly devoured them. I licked my lips. I needed a nap. I could not wait for the next day. Race day. Nothing could hold me back.

Taking Care of Business

Early the next morning, I woke up, eased into my workout tights and sports bra, and then chose an appropriate race shirt for the cool weather. Matt, Jim, and I loaded up the car and headed out to Mackinac Island for the Great Turtle Races. We left at 7:20 to catch the 9:00 ferry in Mackinaw City. Once on the road, we drove through occasional rain showers and watched for deer in the darkness. Matt pulled the car over near Vanderbilt so I could photograph the sunrise. I realized that we should have left the house earlier. I berated myself for poor planning.

In Mackinaw City, the Shepler's Ferry scene was crazy. The lines at the dock snaked down the sidewalk towards the entrance. I had never seen so many people before a race. Since it was also Halloween weekend, many people were heading over to party and not necessarily do the race. The 9:30 ferry looked doubtful, but Jim and Matt remained optimistic.

The 9:00 boat filled up, took off, and the three of us shivered as we waited. Only Jim was in his winter coat. Matt and I were in our race clothes. Miss Margy, our favorite ferry boat to the island, arrived around 9:20. Everyone boarded quickly, and we managed to snag spots on the uncovered top deck. We slid around on the heavy plastic seats, and I felt like a penguin on ice in my black racing tights. Along with the other 280 passengers, a large portion of them warm and happy below, we headed across the water for the 20-minute ride to the island. Since Lake Huron was in a mood, I tried to ignore the white caps and roll of the vessel as it navigated the water. I understood what they meant by small craft advisory.

We pulled into the Mackinac Island dock around 9:50, and the three of us moved quickly through the crowd of people in the downtown area. We weaved our way towards Mission Point. After a brisk ten-minute walk, we entered one of the buildings that operated as race headquarters. Matt and I picked up our race bibs, and then hustled to a separate building where we always stretched before races, put on our bibs, and used the restrooms one last time. Jim met us there and took possession of the backpack. We exited the building and walked as fast as we could towards the starting line.

Runners began the 5.7-mile race first, so Matt edged up towards the front. I stayed back with the walkers. A man named Roy began chatting with me and told me that he was seventy-eight. He pointed towards his "nemesis," Harry, who was the same age. I decided I wanted to be just like them in ten years.

I had always loved the island atmosphere and the camaraderie of the racers. The geography of the different courses, although challenging, brought me back, year after year. I would look for Roy next year.

Five minutes after the runners started, the walkers began. I watched Roy take off like a rocket as he trailed Harry. Although I had promised my family that I would take it a little easier because of my newest health issues, I couldn't stand being stuck behind slowpokes. I reminded myself that elevation was my strength. I navigated the hills by passing people on the edges of the road and cutting in between other walkers while trying to avoid touching them. The sun warmed my face, and the music playing through my earbuds propelled me forward.

I hustled through the curves in the roads and entered the wooded areas where the route split into a mixture of dirt trails and pavement. Slippery leaves and muddy areas were accentuated by horse manure, which was always a concern on carless Mackinac Island. I watched my step on rocky terrain. Roy's blue jacket disappeared around a curve about a quarter-mile ahead of me, and I guessed that Harry was somewhere near him.

After about three miles up in the interior of the island, I worked my way down to the main road that circled the eight-mile perimeter. With less than three miles to go, I spotted a freighter off in the distance. I grabbed my phone and shot a photo. I laughed out loud. Normally, I would never have done this during a race, because I was always too focused on winning or placing in my age group. I started walking faster, swinging my arms as if I was dancing, and passed more people. My head felt warm, so I yanked off my winter hat. Relief.

As I neared the finish line at Mission Point Resort, I spotted Matt in his blue running jacket and white winter hat. He had finished well ahead of me. Then I saw Jim. They cheered me on from the sidelines as I passed by. As Jim shot a photo of me with his phone, I gave him the peace sign. I crossed the timing mat, joyfully raised my arms, and a woman volunteer said, "Don't forget your TRIO medal." Since Matt and I had completed three races on the island during the 2023 season, we would each receive one extra medal.

I grabbed some water and found Jim and Matt in the crowd. We headed to the shoreline for a post-race photo. More racers finished, and the three of us walked back towards the resort. Matt had already checked his results and was 5th out of 28 in his age group. I congratulated him on a job well done. He checked my results and discovered that I was 2nd out of 27 in my age group. "What?" I laughed loudly. I could not believe it. Even after all the years of racing, each top three win made me slightly giddy.

Once again, we headed inside Mission Point Resort where we had picked up our race bibs earlier. I went to the awards table to see what I had won. A friendly young woman handed me a leather necklace, a turtle etched on the wooden trinket. I held it close to my heart for a moment before I placed it around my neck. For the 8-mile race in September, I had been third in my age group and received a plaque. For the Lilac Race in June, I had been first in my age group and won fudge. It had been a good year on the island.

The three of us walked along Lakeshore Drive to the downtown area. We enjoyed a well-earned lunch at Horn's, and then headed to Murdick's to purchase some fudge for ourselves and our neighbor Irene. After grabbing a quick coffee and hot chocolate at Lucky Bean, we walked to the ferry dock, scanned our ticket, and got in line.

I roughly counted the number of people ahead as the wind swirled and a light rain fell. The post-race adrenaline had completely worn off. I was cold.

I looked out across the water towards the Round Island Lighthouse and marveled at its beauty. Mariners depended on it for safe harbor. Several ferry boats navigated around it as they approached the island, one of them ours, and I began to think about the past thirty days. Crazy. I had been unable to speak, had no idea where I was, and I had been blinded by an aura that gave me the worst migraine of my life. I had talked to three doctors, undergone three important medical tests, and felt a whole lotta love (to quote Led Zeppelin) from family and friends as I tried to navigate new terms that were now part of my repertoire. Aphasia. Complicated migraine.

Yet, through my fear, I had explained to my doctors, and basically anyone who would listen, that the race on Mackinac Island at the end of October was extremely important. I needed medical approval, and when I received it, I was ecstatic. I did not tell anyone about the years and years of grief and trauma and how this single race helped me negotiate my darkest days when I was scared out of my mind.

Just before the race had started, I had adjusted my earbuds and prepared my playlist. I remembered sitting in the Delft Bistro in Marquette not that long ago. For five minutes or more, I could not speak, although no one seems to remember the exact timing. I was terrified that I would never be able to say Jim's and Matt's names again. As I stood near the starting line, my bright pink shoes glowed with promise. Adrenaline screamed through my veins, and I thought, *This is it.*

I hit play and left the stain of my fear far behind me.

Acknowledgements

Much gratitude to all of the wonderful people who have given support, advice, and encouragement as I have traveled along my writing journey. I especially want to thank Jim Seitz, Matt Seitz, Chris Giroux, Darcy Czarnik Laurin, Daniel Stewart, Nora Robinson, Diana Burton, Rose Canfield, Helen Raica-Klotz, Elaine Hunyadi, Mary Terzino, Sue Shoemaker, Taylor Parks, and Jessica Tucker. Huge thanks to Ellen Baker, Jerry Dennis, and Laura Kasischke. A special thanks to Dr. Vincent Schultz for helping me during the 2011 Zombie Race when I had a grand mal seizure—and to all of the other people whose names I never learned who also gave assistance. In addition, thanks to Julie Davis, George Davis, Irene Bacsanyi, Jeri Cleverdon, Marlene Glinski, Jeannie Dow, Karen Nentwig, the Michigan Writers Cooperative Press, and the faculty and staff of the Interlochen Writers Retreat. And a huge thank you to Christine Maul Rice for her excellent editorial guidance and for giving me the opportunity to share this story.

About the Nonfiction Judge

Christine Maul Rice's novel-in-stories *Swarm Theory* is the recipient of numerous awards, including an Independent Publisher Book award and a National Indie Excellence Award. Her essays, short stories, satire, journalism have been published in *Allium, 2020 The Year of the Asterisk, MAKE Literary Magazine, BELT's Rust Belt Anthology, The Rumpus, Chicago Tribune,* and *Detroit Metro Times,* among other publications. Rice founded and is the executive director of the literary arts nonprofit Hypertext Magazine & Studio and is the editor of *Hypertext Magazine*. She currently teaches creative writing at Valparaiso University and has served as faculty at conferences, including the Interlochen Writers Retreat.

About the Author

Raised in Dodge City, Kansas, **Melissa Seitz** completed her graduate studies at Michigan State University. She taught composition, literature, and creative writing for many years at Saginaw Valley State University, where she also served as the student editor and faculty advisor of the award-winning publication *Cardinal Sins*. A writer of fiction, poetry, and creative nonfiction, Melissa is also a photographer. Her work has appeared in *After: Stories About Loss & What Comes Next*, *The Bear River Review*, *The Dunes Review*, *The Lake*, *Midwestern Gothic*, *The Walloon Writers Review*, and other journals. She is currently revising her memoir *Lost in Time in Michigan*. Melissa lives with her husband, Jim, on Higgins Lake, Michigan.

About Michigan Writers Cooperative Press

This book was published in the spring of 2024 in a signed edition of 100 copies.

This chapbook is part of the Cooperative Series of the Michigan Writers Small Press Project, which was launched in 2005 to give members of Michigan Writers, Inc. a new avenue to publication. All of the chapbooks in this series are an author's first book in that genre. The Cooperative Press shoulders the publishing costs for the first edition, and writers share the marketing and promotional responsibilities in return for the prestige of being published by a press that prints only carefully selected manuscripts.

Chapbook length manuscripts of poetry, short stories, and essays are solicited each year from members and adjudicated by a panel of experienced writers and a judge who is a specialist in a particular genre. For more information, please visit www.michwriters.org.

MICHIGAN WRITERS is an open-membership organization dedicated to providing opportunities for networking, professional growth, and publication for writers of all ages and skill levels in the state of Michigan and beyond.

MANAGING EDITOR: Gail Wallace Bozzano

BOOK DESIGN: Amy Hansen, Daniel Stewart

Other Titles Available
from Michigan Writers Cooperative Press

The Grace of the Eye by Michael Callaghan
Trouble With Faces by Trinna Frever
Box of Echoes by Todd Mercer
Beyond the Reach of Imagination by Duncan Spratt Moran
The Grass Impossibly by Holly Wren Spaulding
The Chocolatier Speaks of his Wife by Catherine Turnbull
Dangerous Exuberance by Leigh Fairey
Point of Sand by Jaimien Delp
Hard Winter, First Thaw by Jenny Robertson
Friday Nights the Whole Town Goes to the Basketball Game by Teresa J. Scollon
Seasons for Growing by Sarah Baughman
Forking the Swift by Jennifer Sperry Steinorth
The Rest of Us by John Mauk
Kisses for Laura by Joan Schmeichel
Eat the Apple by Denise Baker
First Risings by Michael Hughes
Fathers and Sons by Bruce L. Makie
Exit Wounds by Jim Crockett
The Solid Living World by Ellen Stone
Bitter Dagaa by Robb Astor
Crime Story by Kris Kuntz
Michaela by Gabriella Burman
Supposing She Dreamed This by Gail Wallace Bozzano
Line and Hook by Kevin Griffin
And Sarah His Wife by Christina Diane Campbell
Proud Flesh by Nancy Parshall
Angel Rides a Bike by Margaret Fedder
Ink by Kathleen Pfeiffer
What Will You Teach Her? by Megan Klco Kellner
The Mountain Ash by Kathleen Rabbers
This Blue Earth by Sharon Bippus
Upstairs, Listening by Melinda LePere
Twinkies by Kathleen Quigley
The Sound a Car Door Makes by Natalie Tomlin

Michigan WRITERS

www.ingramcontent.com/pod-product-compliance
Lightning Source LLC
Chambersburg PA
CBHW020443090526
44586CB00045B/832